MW00669122

# *Authentic Hope*

## Experiencing God's Presence Even When You Are An Unwilling Participant

### "Living Life with a Footnote" *

# Mark A. Chrysler

## www.AuthenticHopeforAll.com

Creative Team
Team
Publishing

Creative Team Publishing
Fort Worth, Texas and
San Diego, California

© 2023 by Mark Alan Chrysler.

All rights reserved. No part of this book may be reproduced, stored in a retrieval system or transmitted in any form or by any means without the prior written permission of the publisher, except by a reviewer who may quote brief passages in a review distributed through electronic media, or printed in a newspaper, magazine, or journal.

\* We chose the tagline, "Living Life with a Footnote" because many of our circumstances qualify as "footnotes." We explore these to learn what they mean for each family member. *Authentic Hope* allows us to endure and thrive while learning from, and living with, our footnotes and all they mean for us.

ISBN: 978-0-9855979-4-8
**PUBLISHED BY CREATIVE TEAM PUBLISHING**
www.CreativeTeamPublishing.com
Ft. Worth, Texas and San Diego, California
Printed in the United States of America

**Disclaimers:**

- o Due diligence has been exercised to obtain written permission for use of references, quotes, or imagery where required. Any additional quotes, references, or imagery may be subject to the Fair Use Doctrine. Where additional references, quotes, or imagery may require source credit, upon written certification that such a claim is accurate, credit for use will be noted on the book's website, www.AuthenticHopeforAll.com

- o The opinions and conclusions expressed are solely those of the author and/or the individuals and entities represented, and are limited to the facts, experiences, and circumstances involved. No professional, psychological, or medical advice is implied, stated, or offered in any way whatsoever. You are encouraged to seek professional help, education, advice, and counsel from individuals you deem competent should you desire to learn more about the topics of cancer and drug abuse, or any related topic.

- o Certain names and related circumstances may have been changed to protect confidentiality. All stories where names are mentioned are used with the permission of the parties involved, if applicable. Any resemblance to past or current people, places, circumstances, or events is purely coincidental.

**Scripture References**:

- o All Scripture references, unless otherwise noted, are from the New International Version of the Holy Bible. **New International Version (NIV)** Holy Bible, New International Version®, NIV® Copyright ©1973, 1978, 1984, 2011 by Biblica, Inc.® Used by permission. All rights reserved worldwide.

# *Authentic Hope*

## Experiencing God's Presence Even When You Are An Unwilling Participant

### "Living Life with a Footnote"

# Mark A. Chrysler

## www.AuthenticHopeforAll.com

# About This Book

*Authentic Hope* provides living encouragement to those who have experienced or are currently experiencing difficult times and events.

Sharing glimpses into my life, of living with a young family member battling an addiction and personally living with a cancer diagnosis, is meant to encourage and inspire you. My desire is that you take the most difficult of circumstances and experience God's presence, comfort, and peace through them.

We have learned that God's presence is often best seen when life appears to have handed us the toughest of circumstances. A relationship with Him encourages and lifts us up when we are at our lowest, unable to encourage each other on our own.

To meet my goal of being an encouragement to you, the reader, I chose to share two of my significant life experiences:

1. Living with a family member who battles a drug addiction
2. Receiving a cancer diagnosis which has no known cure

## *About This Book*

As I began formulating what I wanted to write, the simple concept of a "footnote" came to mind. Google has many footnote examples in the definition of a footnote. What caught my eye was "… additional information that would disrupt the flow of the main text ..."

Within the framework of my two life experiences, I think disruption of the flow of my life, which makes up the main text, seems rather fitting. Of course, I recognize disruption is not limited to addiction and cancer.

If you, as the reader, are going through circumstances which may cause your life to have a footnote, this book is for you.

Maybe you're the one reading "About This Book" and your thinking, "Life is good. I really don't have a footnote." That is fine and okay. I believe this book is for you as well.

Most likely you may know someone with one or more footnotes. I am confident as you explore **Authentic Hope**, you will discover tools necessary to help those you know living life with a footnote.

My life is not unique because of my footnotes. Most people live out life with one or more footnotes which impact their life in either positive or negative ways. Moreover, I think the type of footnote(s) or severity of them are not what makes the difference in how one journeys through life successfully.

I believe the defining difference for me was this: my life has been, currently is, and will continue to be focused on Authentic *Hope* as my living foundation as I journey through the challenges and experiences with my two footnotes.

It is true: God's positive involvement with us can best be seen when we have to deal with some of the profound negatives that life can dish out. *Authentic Hope* has been the thread which has been shown to be the silver lining in some very dark clouds.

---

God's positive involvement with us can best be seen when we have to deal with some of the profound negatives that life can dish out.

---

\*\*\*\*\*

**November, 2007:** While waiting for our son to arrive home, the room we gathered in was filled with tension. No one was talking. Looking at the faces of those present to support and love your son, you see fear, anxiety, and contemplation of what will happen next. As the one who is heading up this effort, you reflect on and analyze all the signs and moments when you began to doubt that your son is fine.

Our son was not just dealing with typical teenage challenges. You reflect on the books you've read and the discussions with the so-called experts. You have coached those in attendance and feel confident that your intervention is good to go. Yet, in that moment of confidence, your feet turn to clay. You begin second-guessing the process.

No one wants to believe their child has a problem that requires an intervention. Talk about a self-talk battle, one's anxiety level is off the charts ... then the door opens and Jonathan walks over the threshold into our intervention.

*****

When you ride a mountain bike aggressively, falling off your bike can and will happen. Seven weeks after a minor spill while riding, I found myself sitting in a chiropractor's exam room, waiting for his x-rays to process. I remember thinking, "A broken rib can be painful," but the amount of pain coming from my spine area was, in a word, insane!

X-rays finally came in. Along with a fractured rib, three thoracic vertebrae compression factures were also discovered. Clearly, something else was happening. After seeing several doctors and experiencing too many tests, x-rays, and exams to count, I was diagnosed with cancer: Multiple Myeloma, a type of cancer negatively impacting plasma cells.

As you read and relate, please be reminded that while here on earth we may not know all the answers in the timelines we desire, we can have confidence in God's provision because we trust Him "No Matter What."

*Authentic Hope* looks closely at these two significant life-changing events: a family member with a drug addiction and being diagnosed with cancer. The book invites the reader to experience with the author both tragedy and triumph.

*****

# Endorsements for *Authentic Hope*

As a pastor, I have witnessed offers of hope that seem less than authentic. I served as shepherd to the Chrysler family and witnessed their passage through the ordeal of addiction and life-threatening illness. Unfiltered truth is shared here, yielding thoroughly tested and genuine hope. Read it. Be encouraged!

**~ Phil Herrington: Senior Pastor, Pathways Community Church, Santee, California**

Today, often we're told to "not get our hopes up" because we'll never experience the pain of life's let downs. Mark shows us we can have *Authentic Hope* despite life's inevitable disappointments. Mark gives us a raw accounting of God's faithfulness as he weaves stories from his life, his family's life, and our lives, too.

**~ Todd Tolson: Owner/CEO The Church Playbook**

*Authentic Hope* is a wonderful book of holding onto God's promise of hope amid life and death challenges. With God's help and providence—whether you are battling for your life, the devastation experienced from a family member's addiction choice, or another crisis, *Authentic Hope* is available.

**~ Eric Knowles: Senior Vice President, Shareholder, Religious & Educational Property Group**

Mark and Tammie have been dealt two of the biggest blows a family can endure: addiction and cancer. As a cancer survivor myself and watching my wife's family cope with a loved one's addiction, *Authentic Hope* got us through every day. Mark shares Christ's *Authentic Hope* by being radically transparent, revealing emotions, fears, doubts, and ultimate victory through faith.

**~ Brian Jones: California State Senator, Senate District 40**

# Table of Contents

## Table of Contents

*****

The Author, 2015

# Introduction

My wife, Tammie, and I were married in 1985. Three years later our son was born. Two years after the birth of Jonathan, our daughter Jenna came into the world. The late 1900s and early 2000s was fairly uneventful. My son played baseball and football. My daughter Jenna cheered for Jonathan's football team. My wife sang on the church worship team and I worked with high schoolers at the church we attended.

My son's freshman year seemed to start off smooth. Unfortunately, his freshman year quickly became bumpy. He began to struggle with his grades. He told us he was "stupid," a word we do our best in our house not to use. As graduation day approached for my son, both my wife and I were emotionally drained because of doing our best to help our son graduate. What we didn't realize was our son was in a battle for his life.

I was born in San Diego, California but grew up in a small town outside of Grand Rapids, Michigan. For the record, even though I am a San Diego native, I am a Michigan Wolverines fan and a Georgia Bulldogs fan: Go Blue and Go Dawgs!

From ten years old, I played baseball, basketball, and football until I started high school; my mother mandated only one sport, not wanting my grades to fall. I chose football. After I married my bride in 1985, and after our second child was born, in 1990, I started mountain biking.

Fast forward several years to 2017: I had just returned from a mountain bike race in Monterey, California. While out riding I crashed and thought I had only broken a rib. Almost six months from that crash, I was diagnosed with Multiple Myeloma; a cancer of plasma cells.

Throughout life we are faced with events which have circumstances which produce negative experiences that, if given the choice, we would never choose. However, we all would agree that some events we face control us; control of these events is not given to us. Furthermore, our reaction to said negative circumstances is mostly all we can control. *Authentic Hope* offers a different perspective on influencing our reactions to those negative experiences.

In 1974, at age 14, I sat down with a friend's dad after going to morning Sunday school class at the church they attended, and was asked if I liked the class and what I thought about what I had heard.

After that conversation, I believe my faith journey began. As I grew up into my adult years, I discovered that there are variations to how friends and acquaintances used the word *hope.* Some who didn't proclaim having any faith have used the word *hope* almost like a wish. After saying what was hoped for, there was anxiety with little to no peace their life. Other friends who lived a faith walk into those events which produce negative circumstances, despite their battle, seemed to be at peace.

The Bible describes a different hope, an ***Authentic Hope.*** It is a hope founded on truth from a creator who loves mankind. Together we will explore how one can understand and experience ***Authentic Hope.*** This hope can produce peace, a comfort in life's storms.

*****

Making this book timely, timeless, and relevant to you, is my sole desire, by telling truth and offering practical life applications. I believe that the Bible has answers for us, no matter the circumstances or the questions. To accomplish these goals, Chapters 1-5 of this book will begin with a true-to-life human-interest story, relating to the chapter's theme.

I will then offer a Biblical story that locks in the truths I am trying to convey. As noted, Scriptures are taken from the New International Version (NIV) of the Holy Bible; if another version is referenced, that substitution will be noted, also. Chapters 6 and 7 investigate how ***Authentic Hope*** can influence our perspective on current events and our legacy.

How can we, author and reader, truly discover *Authentic Hope*, no matter what the challenges are we all face in life? I hope to answer that question in every chapter. I am firmly convinced that *Authentic Hope* is available and active for us at all times. Join me in this discovery.

Bike Trail
Photo taken by the author, 2017

> The Bible describes a different hope, an *Authentic Hope*.
> A hope founded in truth.

In this book we will explore these topics:

# Chapter 1

## *Unwilling Participant*

On the morning of September 03, 1965, this five-year old boy awakened, excited with great expectations. I was going to learn to read and write *today*, my first day of kindergarten!

Unfortunately, my anticipations of learning to read and write on that first day were too ambitious, to say the least. Even though my teacher had prepared a lesson plan for our class which undoubtedly included an introduction of elements necessary for a five-year-old to begin to understand what is needed to be able to read and write, I was convinced I would finish the day knowing fully how to read and write, getting it all done quickly!

However, once the reality of *not* learning to read and write that "first" day set in, I decided to abandon the teachers plan and headed out to the playground to play! What I didn't know was that our housekeeper had seen me playing on the playground while school was still in session and had told my mom that I skipped school on my very first day!

Despite that truth, I answered honestly and directly that I was disappointed that I had not learned to read and write and had left the classroom to play on the playground! My mom, being thankful for my honesty yet knowing she had to correct my thinking, told me that I still needed to go to class and give my teacher time to teach me what I wanted to know. On a very fundamental and innocent level, that fateful day I became an "unwilling participant."

*****

You might be wondering why I came up with "Unwilling Participant" for the title of Chapter 1. In 2009-ish, the rehabilitation facility our son was in had reached out to me to say a few words at a fundraiser which allows young men like my son to attend without my wife and I spending thousands of dollars for his recovery, a welcomed financial relief from several other rehabs for which we had already paid.

My first thought was definitely I only had "a few words to share with those in attendance."

At this point in my journey as a family member of an addict, my internal battle was twofold; I was "Unwilling" because addiction sucks, and destroys lives. I was a "Participant" because I love my son and want the best for him. The conflict was intense. I had never been in a position to be face-to-face with evaluating whether or not I would be engaged in my son's life.

Advice from well-meaning people and books on addiction seemed to say that you have to walk away and let your addicted family member hit "rock bottom". There were moments I felt guilt and shame for thinking I may have to turn my back on him.

At this point, I had withdrawn from most conversations regarding our son's recovery. Multiple rehabilitation failures, accompanied by other stinging exchanges comprised of lies, deceit, and theft didn't inspire me with words of encouragement.

However, being a man of faith and taking a moment to quit my pity party of one, I agreed to speak. Leading up to the event where I was to speak, my wife and I would attend meetings intended for families of the men going through the program. Week after week I would hear young men tell their story which, in most cases, were far more devastating to themselves and their family when compared to our story. I believe God used those stories to give me what I call a "checkup from the neck up."

I realized this journey was not about me. God used those stories I heard week after week to change my heart of unwillingness.

In the late 1900s, my family would drive north of San Diego to spend the day with my mom and dad. My dad always had a project going and his project list was kept full by my mom. On one Saturday visit my dad and I were watching college football on TV. My dad was sitting in his favorite spot in the living room on his recliner. As a matter of fact, I think he had dozed off, leaving me to root for Michigan all by myself; Go Blue!

In comes nine-year-old Jonathan waking directly to his papa and begins pushing his shoulder asking what he was doing? Then announcing we all had to get up and start working in the garage! My dad and I had no idea what "work" needed to be done, but that didn't matter: what mattered was seeing my son's face, seeing the joy and determination in his countenance to engage his papa and dad in a work project of his making.

To have his dad and papa participate with him was the ultimate goal for my nine-year-old. Just like we participated in my son's life at age nine, I needed to participate now. My love for my son hadn't changed despite the circumstances.

My mind and heart understood the lessons learned but I still felt unresolved in how to participate in my son's fight for his life against a heroin addiction.

In 2006, our son had graduated high school and soon after that milestone, we (Tammie and I) were strategizing on how to create a drug intervention, which became an epic failure; but more on that later. The real question was, how did we get here?

Junior High School and high school for teens, and parents of teens, are transitional years. I remember arriving to our son's freshman orientation, sitting on the bleachers with my wife, thinking and commenting to her, "We have a high school student!" It was mind-blowing and composed a transition phase for both parents and our new high schooler.

Unfortunately, the honeymoon phase of Jonathan's beginning of high school was short lived. His grades were slipping, and when we discussed his grades with him, with tears in his eyes he would say to us that he was stupid.

We stood before our son, stunned. *Stupid?* In our house that is one word we did our best *not* to say. When alone, Tammie and I asked each other, "Where is this coming from?"

Prior to the ninth grade, Jonathan didn't struggle with schoolwork, and his grades were above average. By the twelfth grade, clearly there was more to the story, but we were in the dark as to how we could help him.

Within a year or so prior to graduation, Jonathan demonstrated behaviors that went well beyond a teenager with self-esteem issues. On some days he would take two to three showers per day. He always carried a backpack with him and was very secretive about what was in the pack.

How he interacted with his family had changed. He had become short, defensive, and allusive. These behavioral changes were 180 degrees out from how our son had lived and loved his family before.

Before long, we found ourselves engaging with Jonathan in ways that seemed foreign to us as parents. Where trust had existed, doubt and confusion had become regular emotions for my wife and I when talking with our son. Quickly, an inner struggle began to take root in both Tammie and me; a pit began to form in my stomach that represented lack of trust, fear of what might be, and the never-ending anxiety of which proverbial shoe would drop next viewing Jonathan's behavior, actions, and breaches of trust. We had no idea then what was about to transpire moving forward.

*****

Since May, 2017 I had been experiencing pain like I had never felt before. After several full body x-rays, a handful of MRIs, and a bone density exam, the diagnosis was osteoporosis. However, both Tammie and myself, along with my primary doctor thought there might be more to my medical story.

Consequently, my primary care physician ordered blood work to hopefully get a better handle on why my bones were breaking. On October 13, 2017, my wife and I went to an appointment with my primary care doctor to learn the results of my blood work. When the Doctor said my bloodwork indicated I had MM (Multiple Myeloma), I thought, "Okay …

I don't know what that is, but I can deal with it ..." thinking, "At least he didn't say the big 'C.'"

When I asked what MM was, he said it was a cancer of the red blood cells. Well, alrighty then. My comfort level completely evaporated. The follow-up proverbial punch was my doctor saying, "There is treatment available, but no cure."

You know that sense of desperation when vision narrows, and sound is blocked except for the sound of your heart beating?

Immediately my mind began analyzing what I had been told by other doctors, that my spinal fracturing was due to osteoporosis. My previous diagnoses, however, didn't seem to completely fit my symptoms. But now I had a new potential diagnosis: cancer. I write 'potential' because I needed a bone marrow biopsy before my diagnosis could be confirmed.

Honestly, my first diagnoses looked good compared to cancer.

You may have heard people say when in an "almost" accident, that they saw their life flash before their mind's eye. On the ride home from my doctor appointment I found myself on the *other* end of the flashback spectrum.

My thoughts were consumed with visions of my son and family coming to my house for a holiday celebration without me in the picture: thinking about my grandbabies growing up without me, their Papa; thinking about not being able to continue on our journey together as man and wife; missing out on future countless moments and experiences which Tammie makes so special.

Unlike dealing with my son's addition, I had no control over having cancer. Cancer became *another* footnote on my life. Interestingly, I still was faced with a decision, similar to the choice to remain engaged in assisting my son to live a life of sobriety. I believed I had two options from which to choose: I could either retreat into an existence of defeat and let cancer get the best of me, or I could willfully make the deliberate choice to be an unwilling participant in my battle to fight cancer.

The Bible talks about a strength which comes from a relationship with God. This is a declaration stating that regardless of the circumstances, in Christ I can do all things. This declaration has proven true time and time again along the way.

Around 605 BC, a prophet by the name of Daniel chronicled an experience that three men, Shadrach, Meshack and Abednego, had endured because of a king who demanded total allegiance and worship from all those residing in his kingdom. Whether slave or free, all were commanded to worship a golden idol or be thrown in a fiery furnace. These three young men found themselves in the middle of circumstances which most of us would not want to be in: to recognize the ruler of that land as God by declaring allegiance to Him as the God of Israel, or be thrown in a fiery furnace to suffer certain death. Shadrach, Meshach, and Abednego were, in my view, living out an "unwilling participant" experience.

In the Old Testament, the book of Daniel records the moment Shadrach, Meshach, and Abednego chose for the last time to not bow down and worship the golden idol. The king, challenged by their refusal to comply with his order, asked the three men who they thought their God was they thought would rescue them from the king's power and wrath for not obeying the king's command to worship a false God.

The book of Daniel 3:16-18 showcases their unshakeable faith, their firm conclusion that whether or not God rescued them, they would *not* worship the king's false God. Through their experience as unwilling participants during the king's testing of their faith in the one true God, Shadrach, Meshach, and Abednego lived out *Authentic Hope.* Their resolve was in a God Who promises to never leave us or forsake us; this commitment allowed them to meet the fiery furnace head on.

The bottom-line truth found in *Authentic Hope* is not based on either a rescue from a fiery furnace, or removal of one's self from any life crisis. *Authentic Hope* is born from the love God has for us which helps us face every trial and test.

> *Authentic Hope* is born from the love God has for us
> which helps us face every trial and test.

In addition to the wisdom found in the book of Daniel, Tammie reminded me that the Bible also talks about giving our burdens and cares to God. She insisted we would be stronger together rather than separately facing the unknown nature of addiction. We resolved to be unwilling participants in the battle for our son's life; <u>that choice became our footnote</u>.

Chances are if you are reading this book, you have experienced the challenge of being an unwilling participant. You know that feeling of "willingness to defy," yet with a "dominating sense of obligation to comply?"

At the core of this book are two life-examples of being an unwilling participant: living with a family member struggling with addiction and coming to terms with a catastrophic health condition.

> **I settled on living my life with a "footnote."**

***** 

Even though our commitment to be unwilling and engaged participants in our son's battle with addiction was a difficult milestone to overcome, the feeling of assurance in our commitment faded rather quickly. My positive identity as a husband, father, family member, and friend were under attack. I had replaced my true identity with worry, fear, and anxiety regarding Jonathan's well-being.

Thankfully, because of my faith, family, and friends, I recognized my first personal battle was to *not* allow my newly acquired footnote to define me. Rather, my footnote was going to provide information I needed so I and others could understand the story of my life.

> ... my first personal battle was to *not* allow my newly acquired footnote to define me.

Make no mistake; this battle was fierce and not over quickly. Along with my wife's encouragement to give my struggles to God, many verses I had been taught in church would come to mind. The preacher's explanation when any believer was faced with frustration, fear, anxiety, and moments of desperation, was that a believer could count on God to never leave or abandon His children.

Additionally, the scripture tells us that God is in control; nothing surprises Him. Even though for us who are a family of an addict, the ring of a cell phone can represent potentially bad news, *Authentic Hope* means God has already seen these circumstances and offers comfort and assurance that whatever message may be on the other end of that phone call, we are not alone.

Deuteronomy 31:8 (NIV)
"The LORD himself goes before you and will be with you; he will never leave you nor forsake you. Do not be afraid; do not be discouraged."

Joshua 1:5 (NIV)
"No one will be able to stand against you all the days of your life. As I was with Moses, so I will be with you; I will never leave you nor forsake you."

> A tough engagement can be the path less travelled.

Faith is the fuel needed for the battle. Much like addict recovery instructions which promote focusing only one day at a time, battling cancer cannot be fought in the future. It, too, is a daily confrontation. True faith produces hope for today, and encouragement for tomorrow, one day at a time.

> True faith produces hope for today,
> and encouragement for tomorrow, one day at a time.

\*\*\*\*\*

Becoming an unwilling participant in a family member's fight for life against an addiction is the right choice regardless of how deep the feeling is of being "unwilling."

Becoming an unwilling participant in a family member's fight for life against an addiction is the right choice regardless of how deep the feeling is of being "unwilling."

*Authentic Hope* delivers on a promise to stand by all who believe. *Authentic Hope* is given when one is in a relationship with Jesus Christ.

*Authentic Hope* in Christ promises to bridge the mighty, fear-laden canyons of doubt and despair we sometimes must confront. And we all have to face them at one point or another.

Rest assured: there is no chasm of hopelessness that trust in God cannot conquer. This hope gives us His strength to endure as an example of God's provision and His faithfulness.

God upholds His word and His promises.

Much like the story of Shadrach, Meshack, and Abednego, three men whose faith did not in any way depend on God *removing* the negative circumstances, we, too must possess a rock-solid faith based on *Authentic Hope.* These Bible characters remained strong because of their commitment to a God who is true to His word. We must have and exercise that same kind of faith.

After refusing to bow down to the king's golden idol, the king ordered them bound and thrown in a fiery furnace. The furnace was so hot that the men carrying the prisoners were killed by the intensity of the heat coming from the furnace.

I can only imagine that the King thought that was that and maybe was about to turn and walk away when he noticed something strange. He inquired, "Didn't we through three guys into the furnace?" Those guards still alive confirmed the act in question. Then the king yells, "Look!"

Despite the flame intensity, the king and those with him who could view the furnace opening, saw *four* images in the furnace. (Daniel 3:24-25)

When the three young men walked out of the furnace none of them were burned and even their clothes did not smell of fire.

What has been and is foundational to my journey with two very distinctive footnotes is not the removal of the conditions which comprised so much heartache and disappointment; my ability to keep moving forward is based solely on the promises found in the Bible which illustrate a God who offers *Authentic Hope*.

> God upholds His word and His promises.

> … there is no chasm of hopelessness that trust in God cannot conquer.

*****

The Trellis Bridge, 2017, Boulevard, California

# Chapter 2

## *Authentic Hope Transcends Experience No Matter What It Is*

Growing up in the 60s and 70s was a challenging, disturbing, and exciting time. America was at war with North Vietnam. I watched the evening news regularly report the number of soldiers killed in action and the number of soldiers missing in action. Hollywood created fictional stories of soldiers captured and abuse delivered by their captors. As a preteen in the 1970s watching fact and fiction unfold, I think for the first time I felt angst over what I perceived the future might hold. Clearly, I would continue to grow older baring any tragic intervention, but I found myself grappling with circumstances which were out of my control yet could impact my life in a significant way.

I am reminded of a story found in the Bible about a young man named Joseph who found himself in a circumstance which was out of his control, and that situation would impact his life in a significant way.

The back story is that Joseph was a slave who found favor in God's eyes. He had lived his life honoring God, which caused him to be in charge of his master's house.

Just when life seemed good for Joseph, his master's wife wanted to take Joseph to her bed because Joseph was a stud!

Genesis 39:6b-7(NIV):

6bNow Joseph was well-built and handsome, 7and after a while his master's wife took notice of Joseph and said, 'Come to bed with me!'"

Joseph's life just became extremely complicated. Giving in to his master's wife's desire to sleep with him would betray the trust he had built with his master and his God. To deny her desire to bed him was to risk her scorn.

Joseph denied her. Because of her influence and deceptions to her husband, Joseph landed in prison.

*****

After my son's graduation, Jonathan was still living at home. Although his behaviors were suspicious, we didn't have concrete evidence that could clearly define what was going on with our son. Mid-week I had talked to Jonathan about working with me on a project on an upcoming Saturday. Reluctantly he had agreed.

At 7:30 a.m. Saturday morning, I was up, had my coffee and breakfast and was excited to spend the morning working with my son. As I was prepping the yard for our project, I asked my wife if Jonathan was up. She reported that no, he was not and furthermore he did not respond when she called out for him to rise and shine.

Hearing the tone by which the message was communicated, I knew I was now tasked with waking up our son. I knocked on the door, opened it, and as I walked through the door I exclaimed, "Rise and shine?!" To my surprise, there was a naked girl lying with Jonathan on his bed; both were fast asleep. Shocked, I excused myself and closed the door! To say I was caught completely off guard is an understatement!

This was an experience that I never had thought would happen in my house. In terms of how to properly handle the situation, I was unprepared, to say the least. As I stood at my son's door, I could hear my heart beating; I was replaying what had just happened as reality flooded back into the forefront of my mind. I thought to myself, "Wait a minute! In my house we do not allow teenage hook-ups!"

One of my biggest challenges in writing my story is finding words to accurately define feelings and emotions. I typically hold in how I feel, which means I have had little practice on associating my feelings with words, to adequately describe inward emotions. For example, whenever I see a healthcare worker and they ask how I feel, my answer usually is, "Great."

In contrast, the feeling of dread that washed over me as I processed what I had just experienced with my son and his naked sleep-over companion resembled playing a game of moves like battleship, checkers, and chess. I felt like I was on the losing side of the contest, and no matter what move I made, I still knew I was going to lose. It was an experience of sheer dread and heightened fear.

Most parents have dreams and expectations for their kids, beginning at their birth. Most parents, I would imagine, don't look at their newborn child and think that their child's future will be saddled with addiction, theft, and dangerous associations.

I was no different. From birth to middle school age, our son was a good kid; he did not disappoint me as his dad. Further, I realized that my job, as a father to my children, was to shield them from anyone who had the potential of negatively impacting them as a bad influence. My job was the protection of my family, as well as being its provider.

As I stood outside of Jonathan's room, waiting for him and the girl to dress and leave his bedroom, I began to realize that my boy could very well be a bad influence on others.

The possibility of my son becoming a bad influence was mind-blowing. Both of my kids were surrounded by a healthy moral environment. They had parents who modeled living life according to the Bible which was taught at a local evangelical church. They had grandparents which re-enforced what my wife and I did our best to live out Monday through Sunday, not just the weekend.

At a young age, Jonathan had a heart for those around him. On more than one occasion he would ask if we could pick up a friend from school and bring him to church. Make no mistake: I am not suggesting perfection in how we raised our kids; rather, we as parents did our best to provide our kids the necessary tools to make good choices.

Standing outside my son's room I went from 'leading' on a board game of moves, to 'losing'. I went from thinking I had a strategy which could see my son through to living a successful life, to confusion and a loss for what move to make next.

If my son was the guy other parents would look at a say, "Stay away from him," then the game had changed dramatically. I was out of my element. I'd had no experience with what we were facing.

Joseph when just a young man was thrown into a hole and sold into slavery by his brothers. As I grappled with the possibility of my son being the influence on others that most would fear and reject, I felt mentally like I had been thrown into a dark hole.

What did I miss? I would question, "Why is my son going down a road that seems to lead to destruction?"

Sometime later after the unauthorized sleep-over, my wife and I went out of town for the weekend. When we were back home on Sunday, I went to the kitchen sink to make tea. As I stood waiting for the water to chill, I noticed something in the drain basket. There I found a Corona beer bottle cap which was upside down making it hard to see. The cap was clearly missed in the clean-up efforts after a party that took place without out knowledge and approval.

As I was getting to the bottom of the chain of events, I discovered that the neighbor kid was part of the party planning. After talking with him, I realized he did his best to keep my son inline so to not overdo it, rather than being the influencer to party harder.

Our son was employed at a tire repair shop at this time. You can probably imagine that working with tires and motor vehicles, one's clothes would become greasy and full of brake dust from changing tires all day.

My wife, Tammie, being the great mom that she is, washed Jonathan's very dirty work clothes along with his regular laundry. At some point she noticed a change in how

Jonathan's work clothes smelled. Tammie brought what she noticed to my attention. My first reaction was this was only grease and brake dust odors typical of anyone's work clothes at the end of a day while laboring in a garage.

I acquiesced to my wife's observance, however, and confronted our son who casually attributed mom's concern as misguided; he claimed the odors were only from working with tires. Unfortunately, as time marched on, my wife's concerns became my concerns because what had been a subtle observation became a pronounced condition. Along with laundry concerns, we witnessed behavioral changes which were changing our son into someone we didn't know.

During the Southern California winter of 2007, the night air was warm, not a cloud in the sky, and the moon was bright. After experiences like our son's exotic sleepover, his physical changes, and stark behavioral changes, we decided to conduct an intervention. On the night of the confrontation, family and friends were arriving with nervous smiles and timid embraces.

After several weeks of discussion, preparation, and prayer, this day of reckoning had come, we were going to confront our son. Hours of researching the ins and outs of how to perform a "successful" intervention had been completed; we "believed" we were ready.

I heard Jonathan's car pull up in the driveway. I walked toward the front door wanting to make sure he didn't slip past me up the stairs and into his bedroom which had become a common move when coming home from being out all day. As the front door opened, my stomach turned into knots. With dry mouth, I asked Jonathan to come into the family room because I had something to talk to him about. We walked side by side into our family room where all had gathered for the intervention.

What happened next became a blur; words spoken were uttered but not scripted. Others present began to interject. What seemed like an eternity was only a matter of minutes.

My heart was pleading, "God, please make this work."

After moving my position from Jonathan's side, back to facing him, I saw fear and flight in my son's eyes. Immediately, he stood up, walked out the back door, climbed over the side fence, and ran out into the street. He was gone — and we had no idea where he went.

Stunned, my mind needed a moment to catch up to what I had just witnessed. Eerily what had been a clear night now became cloudy and overcast. I found myself grappling with circumstances which were out of my control yet could impact our lives in a significant way.

Like Joseph in the Bible account, one must decide on what the next move will be. Whichever decision is made, there will be consequences.

Because of my wife's and my commitment to our son and saving his life, two and a half to three months after that night we found Jonathan and, with his agreement, we checked him into a hospital sponsored rehabilitation. We had no idea if this program was good or bad or whether my son would respond to the process they used.

I still remember the feeling of being emotionally drained as we walked into the facility with Jonathan. After he was admitted Tammie and I, with our daughter Jenna, were walked into a large room with other families sitting in chairs and sipping coffee.

We found three seats together and sat down. After introductions, I honestly don't remember much, other than as other family members, including parents were speaking, certain words were used like 'hurt,' 'afraid,' and 'helpless.' When we heard any of these words, one of us or all three of us would tear up.

As families shared some would break down and cry. When any member of another family spoke and wept, we all three wept with them.

By the time the meeting had concluded, we were emotionally fatigued and spent. While driving home, Tammie began praying, asking God for help and comfort. In her prayer she talked of God's love for our son despite his circumstances.

Like Joseph, we had little to no control over what was happening as we walked through multiple efforts to rescue our son from heroin addiction and all the harm this can cause. However, I believe because we looked to God through our faith, we had a sense of peace in those extreme circumstances.

For example, when a drug dealer was outside in front of our home wanting money for the drugs he had sold to our son, and Jonathan didn't have the money to pay to the drug dealer, I then had a choice to make: don't pay and risk harm to Jonathan, or risk the possibility that the dealer would break into our house and steal the money he was owed, or give the dealer the $250.00 dollars he demanded, and hope that he would then be on his way.

In all my life I had never been in this kind of situation: where I had to choose between two evil, disparaging options. I sought to endure the one that was less evil as I weighed the negative potential impacts on my whole family if the money was not paid.

I paid the dealer.

Like Joseph, foundational to his circumstances in the king's house, Joseph's allegiance was to God first and then the king. *Authentic Hope* meant this: in Joseph's life there was a plan God had prepared for him, and it included the good and the bad as parts of Joseph's growth and development.

Joseph remained steadfast in his choice to serve God, no matter what occurred around him. Because of his commitment and faithfulness to the God he served, Joseph weathered the storm of wrongfully being thrown in jail. He endured.

When reading this story in the Bible, I observe a calm in the midst of the storms Joseph confronted. Similar to Joseph, I found my faithfulness to God critical to weathering the storms associated with living with a treasured family member who had an addiction.

Faithfulness can be described as *willful* submission to a power greater than yourself. This kind of faithfulness is required for anyone to experience *Authentic Hope*.

> Faithfulness can be described as *willful* submission to a power greater than yourself.

*Authentic Hope* becomes the calm in the midst of any storm we endure. Whether in a prison cell or standing in the middle of the street feeling like a failure as a father, God is in control despite the footnote one may have in life.

> Whether in a prison cell or standing in the middle of the street feeling like a failure as a father, God is in control despite the footnote one may have in life.

Proverbs 19:21 speaks of human plans versus what God has declared will take place. Some would say this verse is God laughing at our attempt to set a plan into motion on our own.

> [21] Many are the plans in a person's heart, but it is the LORD's purpose that prevails.

> Because the Lord's decrees will prevail, our successes and failures will fold into God's plans when we put our faith in Him.

***** 

In May 2017, I made an appointment to see my chiropractor. Just one week earlier while riding my mountain bike, I rolled down a boulder and fell into the hillside, compressing my thigh into my ribs. The immediate pain I felt took my breath away as I remained still on the trail next to my bike on my hands and knees attempting to breathe.

At the same time, I was scolding myself for leaving my phone home while riding alone in the back country—not a smart plan. All I could think of was this: the one day I leave my phone home is the day I get hurt! Once the pain subsided to a constant ache rather than searing jabs, I rode the remaining eight miles back home while nursing what I thought was just a broken rib.

After my examination, my chiropractor confirmed: yes, I had broken a rib. For good measure he performed a physical exam from the top of my spine to the base of my spine, asking, "does this hurt" as he pressed on my spine. Each point along the exam I answered, "No, no pain on my spine." A week or so later my primary doc performed the same exam with the same result. Yet the muscles in my back had tightened all along my spine as well as the muscles in my chest.

Almost seven weeks from the day of my mountain bike accident, x-rays were taken of my upper body. To my surprise the x-rays indicated that along with my broken rib, I had three thoracic vertebrae compression fractures on my spine.

I was dumbfounded. I asked my doc, "How could *that* happen?" My fall was a fluke! Compared to previous mountain bike crashes (I have the scars to prove my claim), this crash was soft at its worst. How I had broken my back was a mystery.

However, the pain I felt was clear and without question the most debilitating I had ever felt in my 57 years of living. Life for me changed the day I crashed, broke a rib, and broke my back. I no longer could ride my bike which is tragic being that I am a dedicated mountain biker.

I still worked at my job as an electrical inspector with great difficulty. Walking, sitting, and sleeping were unbelievably difficult activities. Attempting to sleep became an activity that could only be accomplished sitting up in bed at a 90-degree angle, carefully leaning back on a stack of pillows.

After a visit to the doctor which required me to lay down on an examination table, getting myself back to a standing position was quite dramatic. First, I had to slide off to my knees slowly, carefully, then painfully attempt to stand up, getting my legs under me. Walking during this time of my life reminded me of a variety show I had watched growing up, where one of the actors dressed up as a white-haired fireman who shuffled moving extremely slow. The skit was hilarious. When I walked, I *became* that white-haired man who shuffled carefully and slowly.

During this time, I prayed that God would either heal me or help me understand what was happening to my body so I could do something to remedy my miserable physical condition. Again, I found myself grappling with circumstances which were out of my control, yet could impact my life in a significant way.

Fast forward twelve weeks and I was sitting in my primary care doctor's examination room with my wife, Tammie. After several months of pain and suffering we were hoping to get answers and identify a path to recovery. We appeared to get an answer, though the path to recovery was not what we had anticipated.

My diagnosis of an incurable but treatable cancer was not just out of "left field;" rather, it came from the very back corner of the stadium parking lot! After my initial reaction which took place on the inside, Tammie and I walked to the car in silence. Once in the car, we turned to each other and Tammie said, "We got this." Looking back at that moment as I write this book, I realized our experiences with our son had prepared us for what was to come next in our lives.

Understand: I am not suggesting that my son needed to have an addiction to prepare my family and me for my fight with cancer. No, on the contrary, God used an extremely negative and devastating experience to show us His *Authentic Hope* through the perfecting of our faith. Our decision was to either allow the experience to define and destroy us, or to choose to allow the experience to make our faith stronger.

> God used an extremely negative and devastating experience to show us His *Authentic Hope* through the perfecting of our faith.

A cancer diagnosis was a different type of footnote than the one that was added to our lives because a family member battled an addiction. This footnote did not have an external component; the struggle was and is within me.

> ... the struggle was and is within me.

This distinction is not intended to deem one footnote less or more impactful than the other. Rather, I am suggesting my added footnote gave me a new perspective in relating to my son that I didn't have before.

As much as an addict must examine his boundaries and sobriety protocols daily, the cancer survivor living in remission cannot forget the presence of the possibility of the cancer returning.

In April of 2018 I completed a stem cell transplant. After I was discharged and met with my oncologist who was responsible for my transplant, she announced that I was in remission. That was good news to hear!

However, I still possessed the memory of the words from my first oncologist, saying that there was "no cure" and the best we can do is "control" the Myeloma.

My reserved approach in showing emotion or even being able to identify emotions within me, comes from my childhood. I started playing sports at an early age. In the beginning of the season when any sport was offered, if I came home and complained of being sore or had suffered scrapes and was whining about them, my mom would simply tell me to quit. In fairness, what I believe she was thinking was that she was toughening me up rather than pushing me to suppress what I was feeling as a middle school athlete.

Personal strong resolve meant that quitting was never an option for me. From those early days of little league, peewee football, and basketball, I adopted the mindset to stay the course no matter the injury or discomfort. Additionally, I would keep how I felt to myself.

> As much as the addict in recovery lives with the threat of relapse, the cancer patient living in remission also lives with the threat of a relapse.

Hearing I was in remission was joyfully received, bridled with my footnote: it was feelings of joy and reality simultaneously received. When questioned how I felt about the development of remission, I would smile and say, "Good," rather than share that I felt both relief *and* sadness at the same time.

> Not only did I have the assurance of God's presence in my life, but He also said He knows my pain and suffering and offers His strength.

I Peter 1: 3 talks about a living hope (author emphasis):

> "Praise be to the God and Father of our Lord Jesus Christ! In his great mercy he has given us new birth into a *living hope* through the resurrection of Jesus Christ from the dead…"

Though I continued to process my emotions and feelings regarding my diagnosis, the presence of a *living hope*, which is truly an **Authentic Hope** offers peace and comfort *through* those experiences which at times can be difficult at best.

My emotional struggle still surfaces at times. However, my resolve to transcend my negative conditions and circumstances, to celebrations of positive experiences in Christ remains centrally focused and immovable because of **Authentic Hope.** In the verse quoted above, this hope is guaranteed by the resurrection of Jesus Christ. Without that, there would not be true hope at all for anyone.

*****

# Chapter 3

## *Authentic Hope Drives Out Fear*

One of my favorite stories from the Bible is about a young man named Gideon. His story is found in the book of Judges.

Gideon was responsible for threshing wheat collected from the fields. Threshing is a process that separates the seed from a harvested plant.

In Judges, Chapter 6, another tribe was showing signs of war. Gideon was fearful because he felt ill-equipped to battle this opposing army. Consequently, rather than get out into the mix of things, he thought, "I'll just take measures to hide the wheat and wine in the threshing area and see what happens."

Then, an angel of the Lord appeared to Gideon and declared, "The Lord is with you, mighty warrior!" Other versions record the angel saying, "Oh mighty man of valor!"

Have you ever been in a conversation with peers or those you looked up to, and during the conversation someone makes a statement about your abilities in a positive, even "superhero" manner?

My first reaction is to downplay the claim; yet thinking, "Really?" "Could this be true?"

I can only imagine the look Gideon gave the angel, first looking over his shoulder to see if the angel was talking past him, then looking back at the angel with eyes of disbelief. I believe Gideon's lack of confidence in himself caused him to doubt the angel's words in two ways:

1. He didn't see himself as a warrior.
2. He focused on what he thought God should have done in the past, rather than what God *is going to do* according to His plan regarding the Israelites and their adversaries, in their future.

What Gideon didn't realize was that even though we may think God is absent in our lives, often His plans for us are developing parallel to our experiences. God used Gideon in a mighty way despite his fear and lack of self-confidence as a mighty warrior.

> Often God's plans for us are developing parallel to our experiences.

Many times, we are faced with adversarial circumstances that challenge our sense of personal confidence and self-image. Depending on one's experiences we can find ourselves like Gideon, fading into the background, thinking, "I'm finding I am not equipped to fight these battles in my footnote."

In this chapter, we are going to explore how *Authentic Hope* gives us the tools necessary to drive out fear of lack of qualification, especially when we think we may not possess what is needed.

*****

After our failed intervention with our son, who became missing in action for almost three months, the ring of a cell phone became an instant horror show for me and my family. When the phone would ring, instantly we would wonder, "Were we getting the call that our son had overdosed?" "Were we getting the news that he was in jail for drugs, or any other crime typically associated with the illegal drug culture?"

The Bible talks about a father who had two sons. The dad was wealthy and had set aside the inheritance for both boys.

The youngest boy found a way to deceive his dad into giving him his inheritance early. Consequently, the youngest son departed on a Las Vegas-style bender until all his money was gone.

Typically, as this kind of story goes, the son's so-called friends left him and he ended up all alone without any money. He figured his last resort was to go home and hope to convince his father that he could work in the stables for money, room, and board.

When a young family member develops an addiction, even though the Biblical account of the youngest son and my son's story don't match up exactly, both would come to a crucial point of total brokenness before reaching out for help.

In the Biblical narrative, the youngest son travels to his home. Soon he is in view of his family's residence. His dad sees him and runs toward him. Reaching his son, he embraces him, hugging and kissing him. His son steps back ashamed, saying he is not worthy of his father's love.

His father's response was:

> 22 "But the father said to his servants, 'Quick! Bring the best robe and put it on him. Put a ring on his finger and sandals on his feet. 23 Bring the fattened calf and kill it. Let's have a feast and

celebrate. [24] For this son of mine was dead and
is alive again; he was lost and is found.' So they
began to celebrate." (Luke 15:22-24, NIV)

Early on in my son's drug addiction, my family and
I reaffirmed our love for Jonathan by becoming unwilling
participants on his journey. Each time we found ourselves
picking him up from jail at 2:00 a.m. on a weekday, or
discovered him at a place I had no idea even existed, took him
home to get a shower, food, and a trip to a detox facility, we
would have a similar experience that the Bible father had with
his youngest son.

Each time Jonathan felt shame and a sense of not being
worthy of our love. Each time when I could I made sure to
hug him, kiss him, and tell him I loved him. We didn't kill the
fatted calf, but his mom did make whatever he felt he could
eat given his physical state.

*Authentic Hope* can drive out *all* fear. Fundamental to
becoming a beneficiary of living free of the bonds of fear, is to
engage daily in the promises God has given to those who
believe and embrace *Authentic Hope*.

Make no mistake. For those who embrace *Authentic Hope*
found in Jesus, their belief does not rid them life experiences
that can produce fear along the journey. But *Authentic Hope*
brings freedom from the bonds of fear, giving us God's
blessings because of the promises He has given us.

The truth is, there is a counter presence in our world that would love to see us dwell in crippling fear and trepidation. We have a choice to allow experiences and unforeseen circumstances to undermine our peace and resolve; or, like Gideon, we can choose to recognize that God sees us as mighty warriors who can have victory over *any* fear which the evil one brings upon us.

> … recognize that God sees us as mighty warriors who can have victory over *any* fear which the evil one brings upon us.

A second parallel found in the story exists between the father and his youngest on the road to his father's house and our experience with Johnathan. When I find myself doubting or living in fear, bound by crippling circumstances which offer a bondage of fear, rather than trusting in the One who has gifted me with an **Authentic Hope**, I have one of those "check up to the neck up" moments.

I cry out to God, asking for forgiveness for my doubt and for living in fear. What God does to honor my submission is this: *every time* God gives me a special embrace through His Word or through the presence of believing friends who bring words of encouragement and love.

Winning the battle is an assurance of victory over fear. A victory is present to remind me, when attacked again, I *will* win the battle because of my embrace of **Authentic Hope**.

> Winning the battle is an assurance of victory over fear.

*****

Recently I viewed a testimonial where a young girl, ten or eleven years old, with cancer, shared experiences of her diagnosis on an advertisement for the cancer center where she was receiving treatments. She made several statements that for most of us we would find hard to hear.

One statement she made hit home with me. She said, in so many words, that one of the hardest aspects of her diagnosis was *knowing* she had cancer. I recalled that early on, my mental battle of processing my diagnosis was inundated with fear.

When I was diagnosed with Multiple Myeloma, in addition to experiencing anxiousness, I felt a type of dread, worry, and concern I had never encountered before. Growing up, when getting into trouble, I felt similar emotions, anticipating the punishment my father was about to deliver. Though I experienced a dread of the unknown, I knew that eventually I would be past the punishment and fully restored.

When I was told by a doctor that my diagnosis was a type of cancer for which there was no known cure. I became numb. While I don't think I had an out-of-body experience, what I endured at that moment seemed close to it.

Most of my senses seemed to disengage, and only my ability to see was still operational.

Unlike my discipline experiences with my dad, I couldn't see through this new cancer development. With my dad's discipline, I knew all would be dealt with, and that I would be fully restored.

After a minute or so following the initial communication of the diagnosis, my mind re-engaged and began replaying the doctor's words. "Multiple Myeloma, and no cure" seemed to be on an endless repetition in my mind.

Following my first bone marrow biopsy, the results confirmed my diagnosis. The finality of cancer with no cure introduced a state of uneasiness unlike any I had ever encountered, past or present.

For many of life's lesser challenges I had already endured, including their associated fears, I was able to create a plan to overcome them: to defeat the obstacles and dissipate them. However, this health challenge was different. This challenge became a footnote which would remain in my life. Consequently, I couldn't see the other side of this new and highly disagreeable life obstacle. Being told "no cure" presented a whole new hurdle that at first seemed insurmountable.

Every person I had known who had passed away due to cancer, came to mind. Practically every movie I had ever watched where a character who had terminal cancer and had passed away, replayed in my mind.

As I processed those non-fictional and fictional memories of loss, I began to think about what I would miss when I would die. Prior to the diagnosis, I didn't think about dying nor did I think about not being around for family and friends.

Consequently, adding the "no cure" aspect to my diagnosis and the feeling of leaving loved ones before I'd enjoyed a sense of fulfillment in the lives of those I loved, became the composite of a dread-based phobia.

As I grappled with these new anxieties, I became critical of what I was feeling. My self-talk would snipe, "I am a believer, a man of God. How could I be afraid? How could I allow this fear paralyze and dominate my thoughts?"

At some point in the midst of the mental battles in which I was engaged, I remembered a Bible verse that tells the reader to give one's cares and concerns to Jesus because He cares about us.

That verse is in the New Testament:

1 Peter 5:7 (NIV)

"⁷ Cast all your anxiety on him because he cares for you."

It was a verse with which I was very familiar. Now it became a personal confession regarding "casting all anxiety on him ..."

When I was healthy and didn't have the challenge of being a parent to a heroin addict, quoting 1 Peter 5:7 was spoken with conviction and without reservation. I even thought at times, "Why wouldn't I cast all my anxiety on him?"

During that time of my adult life, most personal anxiety seemed to be "low-to-medium" impact, which I believed I could manage, and God was there as "backup," if I am being truthful. Little did I know that my whole life would change in the not-so-distant future.

When we were fully engaged in my son's battle against heroin, those low-to-medium levels of anxiety rose to a level of high and beyond. As I meditated on casting *all* my anxiety on God, I found myself powerless. The mental process I had used in the past simply was not working.

I believe He was showing me that I was *not* part of the solution in casting my anxiety. I believe I needed to tell Him that I was empty and unable to lift my anxiety to Him.

Reality came with a soul realignment. I saw truth. Because Jesus cares for me, *He took the heavy lifting of all my anxiety.* It was only then I began to feel relief.

> Reality came with a soul realignment.

As I was coming to terms with Multiple Myeloma, I was reminded that casting my anxieties on Him was *not* "one and done." In truth, giving God all circumstance of my life became practically a *daily* process, because at times I still felt fear, anxiety, and dread.

The good news is this: God loves each one of us and cares about all aspects of our life. As each day passes, those emotional battles resolve peacefully, one by one.

> …giving my cares to Jesus became practically a *daily* process, because at times I still felt fear, anxiety, and dread.

> *Authentic Hope* is the foundation which validates the claim that Jesus cares for us and is able to receive whatever one may be experiencing in one's life.

Early in 2020, the world became impacted by a deadly virus. So-called experts scrambled to find the science to explain why the virus was released on the world's population and what to do about it. As someone living with a footnote and an immunocompromised condition, I found myself in the "at risk" category. By the end of 2020, my wife and I both had caught the virus. The good news is that by the grace of God, Tammie and I both survived the scourge.

It is interesting how life can take a turn which is totally unexpected, adding circumstances to the proverbial fear bank. The virus concern, to most, was centered on knowing how to safeguard oneself to avoid becoming sick with the modern-day plague.

This newly introduced anxiety in my own fear bank could easily have become a catalyst to stir up those other dormant, dreaded fears and cause the God-indwelled peace already established to become a battleground once again.

However, just as He hadn't forgotten about my struggle with giving all my burdens to Him, God wasn't caught off-guard with the virus, either, and the fact that I had caught it.

The process of casting cares daily upon Him was, and is still, a reliable method.

> The process of casting cares daily upon Him was, and is still, a reliable method.

*Authentic Hope* delivers the assurance that God is never surprised with any circumstances we face. In the Old Testament, Isaiah writes, telling us that God always was, is, and will be in existence. Moreover, he writes that God will never become faint or weary with the details of our lives.

> God is not caught off-guard.

Added to "casting cares" is knowing that God is never on a break, and He will never investigate our lives and become frustrated.

Isaiah 40:28 presents it well:

28 Do you not know? —
Have you not heard?
The LORD is the everlasting God, --
the Creator of the ends of the earth.
He will not grow tired or weary, --
and his understanding no one can fathom.

Jesus had just performed a miracle with a handful of fish and an armload of bread when He told his disciples to get into a boat and sail to the shoreline on the other side. As the disciples sailed, the wind began to pick up, and storm clouds formed.

Keep in mind, most of the disciples were seasoned fisherman who had extensive experience on the water, and had undoubtedly endured rough seas. This time on the water most likely revived past rough sea traumas.

In the middle of the night, a figure approached the boat. The Bible reports that the disciples thought they were seeing a ghost, and became afraid. Jesus called out to the disciples and told them, "Don't fear; it's Me, Jesus." Peter, the more outspoken disciple challenged Jesus saying, "If you are Him, command me to come out on the water with you." Jesus said, "Come." Here's the scripture reference.

Matt 14:28, 29:

28 "Lord, if it's You," Peter replied, "tell me to come to you on the water." 29 "Come," he said.

Peter stepped out of the boat with his eyes fixed on Jesus and walked on the water toward Jesus. As he walked, he shifted his gaze from Jesus and began looking at the storm around him. Peter, sinking now, cried out to Jesus, "Save me!"

Jesus immediately reached out to Peter, pulling him out of the water to stand next to Him.

Living with a footnote is represented in the account as the storm. Jesus is the source of *Authentic Hope,* and we witness His interaction with the disciples, specifically, Peter.

Fear can surround us much like a storm. In any storm, no matter how violent and upsetting, even though we have our eyes fixed on Jesus, we can still so easily turn our gaze *from* Him and refocus back on our footnote. Then the storm cripples us by fear, once again.

Allow me to better illustrate this truth. As 2022 came to a close, unfortunately I contracted the flu from either my wife and/or my grandchildren. Living with my footnote which compromises my immune system, I waited too long before going to the hospital to treat my additional illness.

The consequence of my stubbornness was that my flu turned into pneumonia. My medical condition became dire. This negative condition caused the doctor treating me to put me on a ventilator, a treatment which lasted a full twenty-four hours.

During this time I remained active mentally; in fact, I actually thought I might be facing death. At this instant, I remembered *Authentic Hope* and relived this truth: because I believed in Jesus and the promise of eternal life, I was given and experienced a divine peace, passing all understanding, keeping my heart and mind in Christ Jesus (Philippians 4:6). Before this occurrence, I could only wonder how I might react in such a moment.

At the twenty-fifth hour or so, I woke from the sedative the hospital staff had administered to me, and realized: *I was still alive!* Plus, I was extremely thirsty. Consequently, I pulled out of my left arm restraint and removed the ventilator so I could request and obtain a drink of water.

During this episode, my family had already reached out to friends and loved ones all across the country, requesting prayer. All of them had already wholeheartedly embraced and lived under **Authentic Hope**. It was God answering their fervent prayers that positively impacted me, resulting in recovery. Part of this renewed health included getting the right medication to empower me to experience a truly divine healing. In my view, it was nothing short of a miracle!

What makes hope in Jesus so authentic? It's this: *every time* we reach toward Him to save us from being swallowed up by our footnote, He immediately responds, reaches out, and rescues us. When we are at our weakest, most vulnerable state, consumed by fear that appears insurmountable, we call out to Him, and He reaches to save us no matter the severity of the storm.

*****

# Chapter 4

## *Authentic Hope Brings Comfort and Peace*

> Psalm 119:50: "My comfort in my suffering
> is this: <u>your promise preserves my life</u>."
> (NIV) [Author emphasis]

During the early years of our son's battle with addiction, comfort and peace seemed completely out of reach. The weight of all the emotions encountered when attempting to engage in a safe but involved manner with our son and his addiction would not allow room for peace and comfort.

Several years back, I remember sitting down with a good friend who listened intently as I shared that our son had bolted out of the rehabilitation facility in which he was a resident, and that his whereabouts were unknown. My friend understood that this was not the first time my son had bolted from rehabilitation, and most likely would not be the last time.

After a long pause in the conversation, my friend looked intently at me and stated he had a family member who had struggled for fifteen years and still hadn't found sobriety.

My friend paused to let sink in what he thought were words of encouragement. I smiled and changed the conversation to mountain bikes.

The good news is this: not every day is a dark day. Some days may even offer rays of light showing us a way forward.

Visiting my son and daughter-in-law on the East Coast during the winter months can be quite the experience. In late 2017, we decided to visit Jonathan and his family the week between Christmas Day and New Year's Day. The temperature in Philadelphia was only seven degrees! When we left San Diego, the temperature had ranged from a low of 53 degrees to a high of 70! On the second day back at the B&B from my three-day hospital stay, we got snow.

After bundling up, I walked out onto the porch to survey the amount of snow falling. Interestingly, as I watched the snow fall there wasn't any wind, the snow flurries seemed to fall without making a sound. At this point in time of my cancer journey, I was in the middle of four months for chemo treatments preparing me for a stem cell transplant in March/April of 2018.

## *Authentic Hope*

The view from the porch was East Coast Americana. In the distance were railroad tracks which looked like they had been around for over a century. The buildings on either side of the tracks looked like years of commerce had taken place there. Faded images of price-per-barrel signs, and advertising an era gone by showed ice cold soda pop for 5 cents.

It seemed like a serendipitous moment: no vehicular traffic was present and no pedestrian foot traffic, either. The scene was composed of just my surroundings, snow flurries, and calm.

As I stood soaking the moment in, I was able to experience a respite of comfort and peace. This was a welcomed pause from my weekly chemo treatments. It was a mental "timeout" from all the "what if" thoughts that seemed to invade my space daily.

As the snowflakes fell, there was a sense of going back to my childhood in Michigan. My memory was of standing outside playing with friends, yet knowing the weather was forecast to snow at some point during the day. Then, the snowflakes began to fall.

Honestly, at that point, the game my friends and I were engaged in didn't matter. We all stopped and looked up to see the snow coming down and proceeded to stick out our collective tongues to catch snowflakes. Nothing else could interrupt this.

My snowflake experience at the B&B was genuine relief from all the distractions and challenges of the day. My cancer related footnote seemed to ease into the background, dusted in a blanket of freshly fallen snow. Though treatments were not completely covered in this moment, they were less pronounced. The routine of my weekly chemo treatments and injections seemed to fade. The mental tug-of-war regarding a pending stem cell transplant's success or failure was replaced with calming peace, simply because of a snowflake.

I was confident in a God who loved me enough to send His Son to live a faultless life, to die, and on the third day rise from the dead. This gift offered me authentic hope found only in Jesus. I have had days and will have more of them where I will experience moments like this which may put a smile on my face and become a ray of light, helping to reveal my way forward. This is recalibration of personal thoughts, feelings, and perspectives on the day in and day out of living life.

In 1978, my family and I moved to San Diego, California. It was my senior year of high school. Fortunately, the church we settled on had a large well-run youth program with many teens. There I met a tall blonde haired lanky kid named Sam. Sam and I became friends straight away. As I was getting to know Sam, he shared that he had been diagnosed with Multiple Scleroses (MS). I had heard about MS, but hadn't met anyone with the disease. Despite Sam's footnote, he demonstrated a positive outlook and lived in total reliance on his **Authentic Hope** found in Jesus.

My friendship with Sam remained close into my first year of college. By the time our freshman year started, Sam had transitioned from walking normally to walking with a cane, then a walker, then a wheelchair. Every time I would see him, he had a smile on his face and always an encouraging word for me.

I must confess, I did my best to not focus on his decline but to treat him like everybody else. So, when I would see him slowly wheeling across an open space in the student common area of the college we attended, I would run up from behind him and grab his wheelchair, with Sam in it, and start running.

As soon as we hit max speed for a wheelchair, I would jump up onto the wheelie bars (bars which would keep the wheelchair from flipping over backwards) and we sailed across the open space eventually coming to a stop. Practically every time he would yell at me for scaring him by sneaking up from behind and then would say with his famous ear to ear grin, "don't ever stop, my friend."

Little did I know in 1978-79 that my friend Sam informally mentored me on how to successfully live with a footnote. Because of Sam's *Authentic Hope* living out in his life, he maintained a positive attitude and joy which produced peace and comfort during the tough times.

Mary Magdalene was a follower of Jesus who, before meeting Jesus, was possessed by seven demons and she worked as a prostitute. However, like all others who heard the good news Jesus was preaching, Mary understood and then believed that the message Jesus taught, and her belief in it, would bring *Authentic Hope* to her.

Most people mean well when trying to offer comfort in hopes of bringing peace in times of loss or crisis. Often, however, any attempt to choose right and appropriate words, no matter how noble the intent, falls short.

Years ago, a very good friend and mentor of mine lost his wife to cancer. After the memorial service just he and I were sitting alone in total silence. I struggled to find the right words of comfort to say to him at this time of deep pain and grief. Google defines *comfort* as the easing or alleviation of a person's feelings of grief or distress.

The words I chose fell short and did nothing to provide easing or an alleviation of my dear friend's grief. But even more important than my inability to comfort my friend, was the lesson I learned: a lesson which has been instrumental in helping those close to me understand how to comfort one living with a footnote.

During the darkest moments of either footnote in my life, those close to me had understood for me, the best action was their presence in silent support.

They were engaged in my life without trying to fix or solve my darker moments. Sometimes this meant weeping when I wept. Whether dealing with the heartache that comes from seeing a family member struggling with addiction, living with a cancer diagnosis for which a cure hasn't been discovered, or speaking with a dear friend living with the loss of his soulmate, unless asked to offer encouragement, a solution, or antidote that might address the footnote, offering my silent presence and love for my friend was undoubtedly the better course of action that day.

As I write this book, I have had the pleasure to watch a video production about the life of Jesus during His ministry years. One attribute of the show is the love for humanity demonstrated in the life of Jesus as portrayed by the actor.

Jesus is engaged in relationships with his followers as well as those he ministers to. One scene that comes to mind is Jesus walking back to base camp after a full day of meeting the spiritual needs of those who heard about Him and needed to see and talk with Him.

His mother, Mary, notices how worn out he is and offers to prepare food for him. Barely able to move from hours upon hours of meeting the needs of those seeking him, he politely declines, hugs his mother, and heads for his tent to lie down for much needed rest.

Throughout the previous chapters I have given you the reader's characteristics of *Authentic Hope*. The hope found written on the pages of the Bible is authentic for many good reasons. What speaks loudest to me, is the person named Jesus. I can experience *Authentic Hope* in all situations because of a relationship I have with Him.

My editor and I were discussing Chapter 4 and he pointed out to me that Jesus lived with many footnotes. My first reaction was, "What?" As we discussed the various footnote possibilities, I began to see his point and focused on one footnote that hit home for me.

The Bible chronicles the life Jesus in the four New Testament gospels, Matthew, Mark, Luke, and John. Each account portrays His life from each writer's perspective, but the Gospels are in agreement with each other on the major details.

Jesus was not your ordinary pre-teen. The book of Luke tells the reader that Jesus and his family went into Jerusalem for the Passover festival. When Mary and Joseph were ready to go home, their twelve-year-old son was missing.

After three days had passed, Mary and Joseph returned to Jerusalem to look for Him. During their search, they went to the temple and found him there sitting among the religious teachers, who were amazed at His understanding and His answers.

Mary, despite learning what her twelve-year-old son had been up to for the past three or four days, scolded him for going missing. Jesus, a little perplexed at Mary's rebuke, replied, asking why she needed to search for Him. He said to His mother, "I was in my Father's house."

Most who witnessed Jesus in temple discussing scripture and debating interpretations were, I can only surmise, baffled over this juvenile carpenter out of Nazareth, without any training, who could hold his own that day or any day in the temple.

In the New Testament the Gospel of John, the first chapter, gives us a glimpse into who Jesus is. Because he was born of a virgin, John established that in the beginning (creation) was the Word (God), and the Word became flesh. Jesus was born. In summary, one may conclude that Jesus is fully God and fully man.

Consequently, even at the early age of twelve, Jesus could have been aware that a day would come when He would suffer at the hands of the religious rulers of his day, be nailed to a cross for a crime He did not commit, and be crucified.

In addition, Jesus knew the spiritual condition of mankind was terminal, and the only cure was His death, burial, and resurrection. Without such a sacrifice, the fate of mankind was *without* hope.

Despite such a heavy footnote to live with, Jesus remained positive with those on His ministry team as well as those who approached Him for help. Jesus experienced comfort and peace personally which I believe gave Him the ability to offer peace and comfort to others, throughout His ministry.

Because *Authentic Hope* is foundational in my life, God reminds me of life experiences from which encouragement can result or lessons can be learned.

For example, take the birth of my first grandbaby. Holding her for the first time, and every time after that, produced a love unlike any love emotion I had ever experienced. Not a "good vs. bad" comparison; rather, a love intensity unique to the relationship between grandparents and grandchildren. As my first granddaughter grew, my love for her never wavered. Furthermore, my footnotes faded when I was in her company; her needs took center stage with my focused attention. All she had to say was, "Papa, I need…" and it was done.

I now have three grandbabies, two girls and one boy. From oldest to youngest: one eight years old, one five years old, and one three years old. Each grandchild I held for the first time produced the same emotional love experience as my first grandbaby had.

In the video/DVD series *The Chosen*, Jesus is depicted camping remotely in a wooded area. Eventually, kids out playing stumbled across Jesus' camp. Jesus walked back to his camp and engaged in conversation asking questions that kids would respond to. Quickly Jesus earned their trust, and the children began asking questions of Jesus on their own.

The Bible is clear about the value Jesus puts on children. It warns His followers to not stand in the way of children wanting to meet and talk with Jesus.

Matthew 19:13-14 (NIV)

> "13 Then people brought little children to Jesus for him to place his hands on them and pray for them. But the disciples rebuked them. 14Jesus said, "Let the little children come to me, and do not hinder them, for the kingdom of heaven belongs to such as these."

My love for my kids and grandkids pales in comparison to God's love for me and my family, especially our grandkids. God's love for each of us begins before we were born. In the book of Jeremiah, in the Old Testament, we read the records of God saying He knew us before we were formed in our mother's womb.

Please see Jeremiah 1:5 which says:

> "Before I formed you in the womb
> I knew you ..."

Loss of any life out of so-called inconvenience or perceived necessity, produces sorrows beyond words. If I contemplate a life scenario where I would not have had the experiences of being a Papa, that would be inexpressible pain.

As a man of faith, I believe I have a responsibly to make a path clear for any child, my own, or any other little one, to meet and know Jesus as Savior and Lord.

In the United States, our Federal Supreme Court ruled in 2022 that the Roe vs. Wade decision was not a legally sound one, and overturned this ruling originally made in 1973. With this new ruling, each state (not the Federal government) now rightfully would assume the responsibility to hear from the people regarding how and if an abortion will or will not happen in their state.

I firmly believe that this new ruling by our Supreme Court is a strong step toward clearing the path for more children to find and meet Jesus, just like those kids were shown to have done in the *Chosen* series.

Truly, similar to a profound peace which is manifested in a snow flake, a profound joy is found while gazing into a grandbaby's eyes. In all cases, this joy comes with an accompanying deeper comfort, and a yearning for the lessons which are discovered within the realms of *Authentic Hope*.

\*\*\*\*\*

# Chapter 5

## *Authentic Hope Offers Purpose*

Purpose:
    "The reason for which something is done … Have as one's intention or objective."
~ Google Dictionary

For those of us living with a footnote, maintaining purpose is an action which can easily become allusive to the point of non-existence if circumstances become difficult enough. Regardless of the footnote, what may have been one's stated purpose, can evaporate in the heat of a tragedy.

As I write this chapter, I'm sitting in my office which overlooks my backyard. Just beyond our rear property line is a storm water collection pond. The pond is enclosed with wood fencing that is three tiers tall. On the outside of the fence line evergreens are planted.

The purpose of the pond is to collect rain runoff and divert the water to drain points which empty into a nearby river which connects eventually to the Delaware River. Our neighborhood relies on the collection pond to fulfill its purpose. Failure means risk of flooding when a nor'easter brings two to four inches of rain to the neighborhood during one storm.

A mallard duck and a brown duck just flew into the collection pond area and safely landed on the water recently collected from the last storm we experienced. As I sit and admire the coloring on the mallard duck, I realized another, second purpose for the collection pond.

This purpose is simplistic in comparison to the grander purpose of the collection pond. This secondary, simpler purpose meets a basic need of a mallard duck that is looking to land on water. To the duck, there is no concern as to why or even how the collection pond exists. The duck identifies the collection pond water as a viable place to land and does so.

My neighborhood in Southern New Jersey gave me a structure of purpose to consider. At times, purpose is created to provide a specific outcome. Second, purpose can be instinctual when considering the components resulting in actions out of one's control.

Before being a family member of an addict and before being diagnosed with cancer, my purpose was impacted and constructed by my education, and the life choices I had made. My purpose consisted of faithfully working, attending church, teaching a Bible study, and riding my mountain bike.

When faced with life experiences which are undesirable at best, we can be confronted with challenges that in most cases may seem insurmountable. My assumed life purpose became less focused and more abstract, to the point that my understanding of my purpose morphed into a survival instinct rather than something to fulfill.

*****

For a guy in his 50s, I think I was doing fairly well. In my 30s and 40s, I attended seminars which offered exercises to define mission and purpose of one's career and ministry. Once the objective was reached, short-term purpose statements seem to fade and what became considered status quo took over in the form of an assumed purpose.

First acting as an unwilling participant, then coming to grips with a terminal diagnosis, brought me to a comfort of knowing that my hope is grounded in the Hope within my relationship with Christ.

Throughout my adult life I either attended seminars and workshops regarding identifying my purpose in life, or I taught similar workshops and seminars on purpose, to those who worked for me.

As you are reading this chapter, most likely you may be remembering those kinds of events you have attended in the past.

In the late 1900s, a friend and I attended a business luncheon at a local university. As part of the program, a local business owner would come speak for 30 minutes on leadership, to discuss success stories and provide the audience with tools they had used to become successful.

Often a local pastor would attend our luncheon and speak to us, weaving together business foundations and biblical principles that would support business activities. One session really caught my attention. During this presentation, the presenter/pastor said that what we believe today would most likely not be what we believed in five years.

As the presenter developed his point, I looked at him in disbelief. I quietly scoffed at the idea that my belief system would be subject to any change due to external or internal influences, or both.

Let me set the stage for my experience that day. I'm in my mid- to late 20s. I'm confident in the development of my stated purpose. The framework I used as my foundation of purpose was faith in God. My faith component, foundational to the composite nature of my purpose, was based on one truth: that Jesus is the way, the truth, and the life for all those wanting to relationally know God (John 14:6). I had linked that construct to my overall purpose, leaving my life's operating rules to be influenced by a higher mission.

Before hearing the content of the presentation at that business luncheon, I had firmly believed the certainty of who Jesus was, and what He had come to do. This personal belief was meant to be a firm boundary line, helping to define how I would live my life. I was convinced that anyone who believed similarly would be subject to the same beliefs conditionally, defining had he or she would live his or her life.

This was an established and immovable framework which, to the point of the business luncheon, I thought was a necessary security against whatever life may push my way. I was confident.

On reflection, in my short eight plus years of adulthood, I had never had someone indirectly challenge my belief system, stating that it would change in the following five years.

"How could this be?" I thought, and eventually refocused on the presenter. He went on to state that in business, success often is predicated on how well a business can adjust to changing circumstances. Further, he said that for any believer, there would be moments along one's journey which would have the potential to enrich one's faith if these were recognized as adjustment-type milestones. Additionally, he stated that several variations of belief existed which are defined by circumstances, actions, and responses.

Core beliefs such as the facts of faith described in the New Testament, are singular in intent; they are designed to offer forgiveness of sin and life beyond death. Said core beliefs are the bedrock of **Authentic Hope.**

Leaving that business luncheon, my head was reflecting on his words and my rebuttal arguments. However, once I settled my thoughts, I decided to seek out others regarding such a claim and get their thoughts, perspectives, and opinions.

I am pleased to say that the more I read and discussed his premise with trusted friends, the more I realized that there was some truth to what the luncheon speaker had said. I had no idea that later in my life, the presenter's claim of "belief adjustment" would re-appear within my family, and my life in short order.

**Authentic Hope** establishes and maintains purpose consistency. Eventually, I determined that my core beliefs could and would remain even though an *application* through conviction of those beliefs could change.

The Old Testament contains many stories of men and women who, because of their circumstances, found themselves either relying on their faith to see them through the tough experiences, or they found themselves discovering how much God really loved them, caring for them despite what they were facing.

Consider the book of Job in the Old Testament. Many Bible scholars believe that this book was actually the first book of the Bible ever written down.

Job's story is iconic. A battle of good and evil is played out within Job's life. Leading up to his life being turned inside out, I imagine Job lived with integrity, solid morals, a loving family, and he could have possessed a concluded purpose: living comfortable in his faith and love for God, respecting others who surrounded him daily.

Job found himself in an eternal struggle of good and evil. Job lost his wealth, he lost his family, he lost his health, and he lost his friends. His loss and suffering were so great that his wife demanded Job curse God and die.

Before a personal diagnosis of cancer, and before we learned that a family member was struggling with an addiction, I struggled to see the application of Job's story in my own.

I understood why God allowed Satan to play out what I would call a fool's errant attempt to break Job. But the devil was up against an omniscient deity. God knew Job and He knew the outcome of the battle being played out in Job's life.

God foreknew, regardless of what was done to Job, that he would remain a faithful loving servant of God, as he had been before the traumas first occurred.

Living my life with two distinctive footnotes, studying Job's life, has brought new meaning to why God not only allowed the devil to attempt to wreck Job, except taking Job's life.

God determined that this story was important enough to be put in the Bible for countless generations to read and ponder. We consider this story now to learn why the account was related for us to read, and from which to learn.

We can identify with these significant components of Job's life:

- Job was successful in business and wise in his family decisions leading up to the devil taking note and challenging Job's faith before God.
- Job did nothing to warrant the increased destructions the devil threw at him with the goal of getting Job to curse God.
- Job remained faithful even when others wanted Job to renounce his faith and curse God.

I believe Job's story illustrates to us how any footnote that is established isn't critical to the outcome of one's story.

> … Job's story illustrates to us how any footnote that is established isn't critical to the outcome of one's story.

Some footnotes may be established because of choices we make. Some footnotes are established by those around us, over which we have no control. Some become established through external influences. Regardless, they are still present. Job's battle is comprehensive enough that any reader can see the footnotes in his story and how he dealt with them. God rewarded Job's faithfulness. He will reward ours, too.

The final outcome of Job's story is possible for us when we battle evil and remain true to our personal *Authentic Hope.* Those of us who possess living faith in God and choose to remain faithful no matter what, even when a family member struggles to maintain sobriety, and even when we may be diagnosed with terminal cancer though living in remission, we choose to continue to trust God and His will.

We conclude this: our faithfulness will remain steadfast, sure, urgent, and sincere when we battle for a family member's life, or our own existence.

> … my core beliefs remain even though an *application* through conviction of those beliefs could change.

*****

# Chapter 6

## *Authentic Hope in Current Events*

### Social Media

In 2022, social media has all but taken over physical discourse in most modernized cultures where WI-FI internet is available. Whether one texts others to communicate, or records short clips of what seems to be the trend of the day so others can participate, this electronic form of communication is used extensively. The message is received without personal interaction.

In contrast, consider a boy born in the early 1960s. Socialization was accomplished on a single cranked two-wheel bicycle riding through the neighborhood looking for kids with whom to play. Despite the stark contrast of the 1960s, when compared to 2022, *Authentic Hope* can be found and is, or can be, effective in an engagement of social media.

I am a member of the Baby Boomer generation. Consequently, I believe I have a unique perspective about the evolution of social media because, as a child of the 60s, I witnessed the start of the internet. In the beginning of the social media platforms, if you were to log on, you might see pictures of events like birthday parties or graduation parties, to name a few examples of what might seem post worthy.

Eventually, I remember one platform that seemed to encourage those who signed up, to participate by relating "all" the activities one may take when waking up in the morning. In those early developmental stages, people were recording and publishing their every movement.

For example, "I woke up, I brushed my teeth, I am walking to the kitchen to eat cereal ..." As other platforms emerged, the information flow changed from step-by-step documentation of one's life, to more generalized messaging.

Engaging in a social media culture while living life with a footnote, can be helpful and challenging at the same time. When face-to-face and live interaction occurs, you can read the persons physical reactions to what is being discussed. In contrast, posting your message on a social media platform, the ability to notice physical reactions to what your message is communicating to the person reading your message, is lost. Consequently, I believe messaging becomes critical to not only the receiver(s) of your media post, but the message composite also becomes critical to you, the sender, as well.

For the record, I am not turning this chapter into a "how to" message for effectively engagement in social media. My objective is to explore use of messaging with a <u>purpose</u> which can improve one's experiences in messaging, and ultimately protect the sender of the message.

By 2022, social media messaging and media messaging in general dramatically changed in comparison to the early 2000s. For years the joke around the office water cooler was if you want the answer to a question, check the internet, you can't go wrong. Of course, the last statement was expressed tongue in cheek.

At first the population embraced the internet as a reliable source of needed information. However, the veracity of the information made available was severely lacking. The difference is this: in today's culture of social media, there are some who willfully post messaging that purposely intend to mislead for a specific gain. Consequently, the recipient of messaging created in social media and messaging created by most news media outlets, has a formidable task of determining whether the message is authentic, trustworthy, and dependable.

As I stated early in this section, **Authentic Hope** *can* be found in one's social media engagement. When messaging has the potential to mislead, deceive, and corrupt the receiver, I believe the receiver needs a strong foundation which will be necessary to with stand messaging that is not authentic.

In my experience with social media, one axiom that is important to understand is this: not all that is positioned as truthful is truth.

- o **Truthful**: "Telling or expressing the truth; honest."
  ~Apple Dictionary
- o **Truth:** "The quality or state of being true."
  ~Apple Dictionary

Prior to the internet and the ability for anyone to post a message online for all to see, media was confined to print and network platforms. Print media had reporters who found a story, vetted the source for reliability/truthfulness and then published with their name attached. Network reporting was a similar process, but ABC, NBC, and CBS would hire a News anchor to read the news for their audience who tuned in to watch the news.

When reporting was met with criticism there were ways to challenge the report. Ultimately, because the pool of those reporters engaged in looking for the event and or story, was limited, the ability to manage truthfulness seemed easier to maintain. In the late 1900's into the new millennium, a shift began to form regarding what could be posted even though some messaging did not appear truthful.

In my view, what increasingly became apparent was that the pool of "reporting participants" had grown way beyond what was in place before the internet was created and made available to anyone who owned hardware to access the world wide web.

When George W. Bush became the 43rd President of the United States, the online attacks on him were nonstop. Rather than criticize policy decisions, those writing began attacking the person.

After reading some of those personal attack posts I felt concern for our country. By the end of 43's time in office, their seemed to exist a concerted effort to personally destroy President Bush's character with no regard to truthfulness; what was being messaged in print, network, and social media was far less than truth.

My concern elevated to heartache. Lines seem to have been drawn. Respect for the Office of the President seemed non-existent if a republican held that office. Clearly, any American who values our nation and pledges loyalty to our flag as "One nation under God" needs *Authentic Hope*. Established truth is true north.

> Established truth is true north.

The core of *Authentic Hope* _is_ truth. God, as described in the Bible, _is_ truth. Fortunately, what our nation has experienced over the past two decades is not a surprise to God.

Jesus lived on this mortal coil for approximately 33 years. During that lifespan, He taught and showed us how one can have a relationship with God in spite of difficulty. He said, "I am the way, the truth, and the life. No one comes to the Father except through me." (John 14:6, NIV)

People in personal conversations with Jesus asked many questions of Him. Through those discourses, they were deciding if Jesus was truthful. They wondered, "Could He be trusted?" Because of who Jesus claimed to be, one vital and life-changing truth He declared was about how to have a relationship with His Father in heaven.

Those of us who have embraced *Authentic Hope* have a working understanding of real truth because of this: regardless of any social messaging to which I am exposed personally, my faith and hope are based on the Gospel message which was validated the moment Jesus defeated death and established Himself at the right hand of God.

So, let's discover how to apply *Authentic Hope* in a social media experience. I'll use me as an illustration.

My social media involvements are limited by choice. I message on two platforms only. With my schedule, two platforms are manageable.

My messaging consists of posts that I vet, and I know them to be truthful. A plethora of other posts may be enticing;

however, I was taught years ago this additional life truth: "never attempt to wrestle a pig in the mud. Pigs love mud and you will lose!"

## Politics

There may not be a quicker way to start an argument at the dinner table than discussing political issues of the day with those who may not share the same views that you do.

Politics of the day can be consuming depending on one's concern for our Republic. I would consider myself a patriot and I do share this concern. My attention to political news and commentary can at times be consuming because of the real-time impact being made.

Not all people are interested in politics. Over the years I had developed a moderate interest with minimal engagement. When our first Afro-American president was elected in 2008 and was sworn in, in 2009, his primary campaign promise was his commitment to "transform" America. As his first year unfolded, his goal to transform America meant to fundamentally alter the work our founding fathers had put in place with documents like the Constitution and Declaration of Independence. Once I understood what President Obama meant by transform America, I felt uneasy.

*Improve* America, and I'm all in. But to *transform* means to modify what exists into something different. My interest in politics was no longer moderate. My attention shifted because political circumstances dictated increasing importance and potential impact severity.

*****

In my experiences, despite the importance of what may be going on politically, when a family is faced with a family member battling an addiction, news of the day tends to fade into the background and all focus is on the family member with the addiction. Similarly, when an individual is faced with a terminal cancer diagnosis, the news of the day isn't in primary focus, as one grapples with what the diagnosis means and how life will look moving forward.

Refocusing attention away from current events toward a footnote is understandable and expected. I am not suggesting that what happens on a political front isn't important and/or critical to the survival of our Republic, the United States of America.

Rather, I am suggesting that despite the critical nature of what is reported regarding those we voted into office, my experiences have shown me that my *ultimate* focus should be founded first on *Authentic Hope*, our footnote(s), and then on noteworthy topics or actions like politics.

From an early age, I was sensitive to half-truths and outright lies. For example, I have the mind that allows me to process a bit quicker than most people I encounter regarding what is being discussed. This trait worked well when I represented employees in a labor dispute with the municipality for which we worked.

However, this trait of mine did not work well when I moved my focus toward politics in a consuming manner. When Mr. Trump won the election in 2016, those opposing him began to unload ruthless attacks and accusations upon him, his family, reputation, and cabinet. Even before he was sworn in, January of 2017, many of the Democrat opposition, including the mainstream media were claiming the election was rigged and he was not the legitimate winner of the election.

I recall thinking that if Mr. Trump won, the attacks 43 endured to date had been the worst a republican president would get while in office; unfortunately, I was wrong.

As I observed in the social media section above, finding truthful messaging in the current political arena has become increasing more difficult. Unfortunately, those who currently hold the power to set policy have what appears to be a commitment to openly "gaslight." That term means: "manipulate someone by psychological means into questioning their own sanity." ~ Apple Dictionary

At least half of the population in the United States are constantly exposed to this kind of manipulation. Messaging from the gaslighting camp is not only untruthful; it is also purposely deceitful and evil.

When this is the case, should my focus land squarely in the conflict to discover truth and weed out lies, I begin to experience anxiety and despair. When I shift the majority of my attention to politics, it is then I began to erode my foundation found in my *Authentic Hope.*

Because I have lived for years with *Authentic Hope* in my life, I realize quickly: <u>I need to move my attention away from a created mess of messaging and deliberately focus on the Creator of Life in truth and love.</u>

As I have said in previous chapters, I give myself a checkup from the neck up.

The good news is that *nothing* changes regarding what God brings to my life. His provision is constant, and centered in His Person, who is *truth.*

Please see James 1:17 (NIV):

> 17 Every good and perfect gift is from above, coming down from the Father of the heavenly lights, who does not change like shifting shadows.

Indeed, if any changes occur, they are all on my end.

## World Events

As a junior in high school, I must confess I really enjoyed going to a person's house with several of my buddies. Who may have lived there didn't really matter, but in an effort to give full disclosure, the person living at the house was typically a girl one of us liked. We had 100 rolls of toilet paper that needed to be thrown into the trees on the front lawn of the house. When we were finished on that cool fall night, the house looked like it had just snowed, with mounds of toilet paper coating all the branches with this white material. Of course, as was expected, the dad usually would come and yell that he had called the police and we were in big trouble!

As we hid from the police car and search light, we never thought of the police as the enemy. We respected the police even though we successfully hid from them and we were able to strike again on a future night before winter set in.

During the sixties, of course, there were examples of police brutality as well as other individual actions by members of a police force that were unlawful, not right, and certainly not appropriate. I believe society, for the most part, saw those actions and dealt with those responsible.

Pressing forward to 2020-2021 a movement began against all police that no longer focused on those individuals who were wrong in how they carried out their sworn duty. Rather, the public discourse used a broad brush that criticized and condemned, and in some cases sought to defund all practitioners of law enforcement.

Most of the reporting media fueled the statements and stories, trying to demonize law enforcement with disinformation. Taken to an extreme level, riots could break out, and when they did, innocent law enforcement members could be brutally murdered.

Another example willful disinformation was found in a Reuters article dated July 26, 2022, "No, we're not in a recession," the Biden administration tells U.S. voters. Interestingly there are those in the Administration who just four to six months ago made statements on video analyzing the economy, stating that when two consecutive downward trending quarters occur in Gross Domestic Product (GDP), we would be moving into a recession.

Apple dictionary defines recession: "A period of temporary economic decline during which trade and industrial activity are reduced, generally identified by a fall in GDP in two successive quarters." Yet, our current administration wants to convince us that we have a strong economy and wants Americans not believe the empty shelves at the grocery store, high gas prices, and climbing energy costs.

Sadly, willful disinformation from leaders of the day is not a new occurrence or problem. Around 30 AD the religious leaders of the day were determined to not only shut down the discourse of a man named Jesus, but they were also determined to kill Him because He taught a message of forgiveness and eternal life.

Ultimately, their plan was carried out by putting Jesus on a cross for execution. The good news is that Jesus defeated death on the third day after being laid in a borrowed tomb. <u>His resurrection became the foundation to *Authentic Hope*</u>.

There is an ugly parallel that may exist for you, the reader, and me, the author, who also is a family member of a person battling an addiction. Unfortunately, an addiction often drives the addicted person to obtain monetary resources that may be available. This translates to jewelry, valuable collections, and power equipment just to name a few examples of tangibles taken to be sold or melted for cash

What strikes even harder are the lies told, and the deceptions and false pretenses perpetrated to maintain the addiction. Consequently, when our elected governmental officials display behavior distressingly similar if not spot on to behaviors of an addict, the red flags go up!

Focus on the effort by our federal government to gaslight the American public. This is one of the go-to tools of an addict: to try to convince family that what they are experiencing and to which they fell victim were not real and everything is okay.

Despite what is happening in our world, ***Authentic Hope*** offers strength to withstand the constant onslaught of disinformation.

Social media, politics, and world events, while important, are simply not as vital to life and health, nor in any way can they "replace" ***Authentic Hope*** and our trust in the God who gave us that hope. ***Authentic Hope*** is true always. God is worthy of first place over all social media, politics, and world events, be they true or false or somewhere in between.

When ***Authentic Hope*** is the bedrock of one's resolve in relation to any footnote, influences like social media, politics, and world events will not upset your **faith balance**. Abide in ***Authentic Hope*** and your ability to maintain balance and prospective is greatly enhanced.

*****

# Chapter 7
## *Authentic Hope and Your Legacy*

In this chapter, we will consider these points:

1. How you see others' legacies
2. How you see your legacy
3. How others will see your legacy

> **Legacy**: "The richness of the individual's life, including what that person accomplished and the impact he or she had on people and places. Ultimately, the story of a person's life reflects the individual's legacy."
> ~ Apple Definition

Thinking back over the years of my adulthood, my exposure to the meaning of legacy was often defined by fictional stories found on television. On any given program, typically the plot involved a political candidate who was determined at any cost to create his or her legacy that would be recorded in history as someone who accomplished something great to benefit mankind.

Inevitably, in the efforts to establish the main character's legacy, however, ethics needed to be compromised to meet the actor's legacy goal.

Fortunately, the fictional tale is just that, fiction.

In the mid to late 1960s my mother had divorced my birth father because he had become an out-of-control alcoholic. Mom and I relocated temporarily to my grandmother's home (Gram's house) in Kalamazoo, Michigan. My mom had met a guy she thought might be the one she would introduce to me. Unfortunately for this gentleman, my mom also became acquainted with a man named Dave Chrysler. This introduction was made by my uncle, Chuck.

Well, I liked Dave a *lot*. While on a date with the *first* guy, I began asking mom if she liked Dave. I stated quite forcibly that I *really* liked Dave. After that, mom let the "other" guy down gently.

Dave raced motorcycles with my mom's brother, Chuck. In 1968, Dave was considered number one in points and my uncle Chuck was a close second in the TT (Tourist Trophy) racing class points standing.

Not long after that season, Dave and my mom were married. From the start of their union, I considered Dave to my dad. Quickly, I realized that there wasn't anything I could break, and dad could not fix. If I needed something made, dad could make it.

As I aged, I began to see that I wasn't the only one on the receiving end of my dad's talents. His skills extended to the automotive industry and house construction. Pick any trade, and he had a working understanding of it.

For the record, when I would swing by his house from time to time and look around his garage at the electrical wiring he would install and use, my dad often would give his electrical inspector son a smirk smile asking, "What, it works?"

My dad was never boisterous about his talents; rather, when discovering a need, he either completed the task himself or recruited me and others to get the work done for those who couldn't do for themselves.

My dad passed away in 2013 from lung cancer. If his life account was limited only to his mechanical skills, then his legacy would be rich with those who benefited from knowing Dave Chrysler.

In the mid-1970s, dad had arrived at an existential crossroads. Was he going to allow his footnote, alcohol, to control him, or was he willing to embrace the gospel account of who Jesus was on this mortal coil and who He was and is today after defeating death? Fortunately, dad chose life. He recognized the need for **Authentic Hope** in his life. Not long after that milestone moment, he began reaching out to others battling personal footnotes, offering support and affirmation.

Many men were familiar with my mom and dad's home which had a nook where coffee was consumed, and tears were shed as my dad shared his life and how he now embraced **Authentic Hope** in his life. This was a hope for the asking, that any person could possess and enjoy.

My legacy development potential shifted to a positive skew because of my dad. He modeled a strong work ethic, the importance of a man's word and, in all circumstances, he demonstrated that truth and integrity must be the tools used to determine life's decision outcomes.

His legacy that was both temporal as well as eternal. In the end, the houses, cars, and hot rods he built would fade away, but the lives he influenced to consider and embrace **Authentic Hope** will last an eternity.

> That was, and is, his legacy.

In the late 1900s, circa 1984, I met Lamar Johnson, who was my girlfriend, Tammie Johnson's, father. He owned an electrical contracting company. On a soggy day after a rainstorm, I was in a trench shoveling out mud to eventually allow others to bring in piping for a sub-division to be constructed in Santee, California.

Around lunch time I looked up and saw Lamar standing at the trench edge, asking me if I liked what I was doing for work. I said grateful for what I have but always looking to improve. Lamar had already cleared an absence with my site supervisor allowing me to go with Lamar, and grab a carne asada burrito. Well, that lunch changed my life.

I worked to become a journeyman electrician under the banner of Johnson Electric. Lamar re-enforced all the work and life lessons taught me by my dad, and he added more. During the time I spent working at Johnson Electric Company I was taught many life-impacting lessons which served me well as I moved on working for larger electrical contracting companies. Eventually, my experience and knowledge of the electrical trade helped me secure a position with the City of San Diego.

On January 2, 1991, I began working with the City of San Diego as an electrical inspector. Our chief electrical inspector reached out to me one day and encouraged me to check out an organization that held meetings with all electrical industry professionals. I did this and joined the International Association of Electric Inspectors (IAEI). My association with IAEI afforded me the opportunity to be part of the education effort to all those who attended IAEI meetings. Providing education to attendees gave me the satisfaction that I was investing into the electrical industry professional's future. Because of my training and teaching experience, eventually I promoted to Senior Electrical Inspector for the City of San Diego's Development Services Department.

Further, because of my association with IAEI, I was able to serve on the National Fire Protection Agency (NFPA) code making panel 14 for NFPA 70, the National Electrical Code for the 2020, 2023 code additions.

In fact, I remain an active member of IAEI even into retirement. In 1984, because my future father-in-law decided to visit my jobsite and offer me a chance to learn a trade in the electrical industry, I was able to accomplish more than this trench construction laborer could have ever imagined, and I will forever be grateful. Lamar's legacy doesn't stop with me. His investment is tracible in many young men who began working for Johnson Electric as an apprentice electrician.

In 1974, after attending church and discussing what I had heard with a family friend, I decided to become a teenager of faith. As I grew in age, my faith grew as well. Eventually, I became a man of faith, developing an understanding of how the truth of *Authentic Hope* would impact my life in positive ways, even though severe and dark times would beset my life in the future.

My faith journey was comprised of church influences where, in my senior year of high school, the youth pastor of the church I attended appointed me to the student leadership team. My experiences qualified me to work with a parachurch ministry called Campus Life, as a school director. As a matter of fact, I met my editor/publisher at my first concert ever conducted by Campus life.

I then left ministry to venture out on a business dream I had envisioned. Unfortunately, that dream died due to loss of silent partner funding.

After meeting the lady who was to become my wife, Tammie, we married March 30th, 1985. In 1988 our first born entered our world. A friend from church was working toward ordination and asked if I would help him with the high school program. That experience spring boarded me into a volunteer youth director position with a church in Santee, California, for nearly eleven years.

Ministry with high school students was most rewarding because I was afforded the opportunities to have influence in students' lives. When I worked with Campus Life, the model used for student influence was this: that positive impacts could be made on physical, mental, social, and spiritual levels. When I transitioned to the youth director position, I carried that example with me. This way of ministry produced significant life impact in the lives of the students with whom I worked.

Consequently, I see my legacy as *someone who is driven to invest in others*. Early in my life I was told that my name, Mark, meant "a defender of those in need of defending." Whether or not that definition is true, those words resonated with me then and through the many years preceding and following that moment to the present.

First and foremost, I purpose my actions to be defined by my conviction. I firmly believe that helping others is more important than any accomplishments and titles I may have acquired. Honestly, thinking about my legacy is secondary to my commitment to investing in others' lives.

I believe one contributing factor to maintaining the integrity of one's conviction is the commitment to learn from others and understand *their* footnote. When I can see change for the good in the lives of people I meet and when eventually I interact with them, it is then I think my legacy is on the right track.

When Jesus ministered on this mortal coil, He taught His followers, as well as those who came to hear Him speak, that fulfillment of the laws practiced long before his birth are fulfilled by loving others. As one loves himself or herself, that person demonstrates loving God exclusively through loving others.

One establishes sincerity in loving God by fully embracing *Authentic Hope*. This sincerity is grounded in a very real and personal relationship with Jesus Christ. Despite all the ups and downs recorded in this book, despite the footnotes which, in most scenarios, contribute greatly to the down portions of my own life's experiences, *Authentic Hope* provides calm in all of life storms, and God's peace especially when understanding may be hidden in moments of despair and anguish.

*Authentic Hope* does not remove the footnotes, or the down experiences one may face. However, the relationship with God formed out of *Authentic Hope* gives us Joy in *all* circumstances. This is true because of a promise God made and constantly fulfills: that He will *never* abandon us in good or up times, and in bad or down times.

I once heard of an evangelist who, when interviewed, was asked about his death. The question was this: when he died and stood before God, would he hear, "Well done good and faithful servant." At the time of this interview, this evangelist had preached to millions of people in stadiums which were broadcast nationally and internationally. Thousands had embraced the message found in *Authentic Hope* and had started a personal relationship with God. His reply to the question was, "I don't know."

I thought long and hard about that interview. Eventually, I believe his mission was clear: it was to reach as many as he could, to tell all who would listen that there is good news found in a relationship with God, and His Son, Jesus Christ. I believe his answer was grounded in humility.

When those who know me and judge my legacy, I hope I am viewed as someone who loved others enough to invest in their lives by first demonstrating what life looks like with **Authentic Hope**, then be willing to share what **Authentic Hope** means.

*****

# Credits

Please join me in recognizing and thanking these wonderful contributors to this project.

1. <u>Tammie T. Chrysler</u>: *"Support"* Without my wife's calming spirit and commitment to prayer, I am not sure I would have made through the addiction part of my/our story let alone write a book. Tammie, my better half, I love you.
2. <u>Jonathan M. Chrysler</u>: *"Permission"* Before writing began, I talked with my son about my goals for the book and inquired if he was comfortable with those goals. I asked him if I would I have his permission to write his part of this story. He said yes. Jonathan I am proud of you and your passing a five-year sobriety milestone, I love you.
3. <u>Jenna R. Chrysler</u>: *"Perseverance"* Rosebud, your patience and determination to see our family remain whole is commendable. I will be forever grateful for your support of mom and me during the dark years of addiction and now as I battle cancer.
I love you.

4. <u>Glen Aubrey</u>: *"Encouragement"* Thank you, Glen, for believing in me all the way back to that concert we worked for Campus Life's Breakaway at Point Loma College. To convince a guy that his story must be told and be patient enough as I stumbled through my writing process, is a small miracle. Thank you for your friendship my brother.

I love you.

<u>Five Important Individuals</u>: *"Undergirding"* Listed below are friends who have embraced **Authentic Hope** in their lives. Each man has a very different story from the others, but each one has consistently been there for me during my journey through my son's addiction and my battle with cancer. Gentlemen, your impact in my life is hard to put into words, but please know this, I love you.

Adam Ferris: Master carpenter/builder
Eric Knowles: Senior Vice President, Shareholder
      Religious & Educational Property Group
John Bayliss: Senior Electrical Inspector for San Diego County Regional Authority
Brian Jones: California State Senator
Kurt Brickley: Multiple trade Inspector for the Port of San Diego

# Products, Services, Resources

**Products:**

*Authentic Hope*: www.authentichopeforall.com

**Creative Team Publishing (CTP)**:
www.creativeteampublishing.com
This is the location where you can purchase *Authentic Hope* and other CTP books.

**Services**:

**Genesis Recovery, San Diego**:
https://www.genesisrecovery.com
**Sydney Kimmel Cancer Center, Sewell, Philadelphia**:
https://www.kimmelcancercenter.org/cancer-center.html

**Resources**:

*New American Standard Bible* (Nelson, Publisher). https://www.thomasnelson.com

*Christian Standard Bible* (Holman, Publisher). https://www.bhpublishinggroup.com

*Lincoln's Leadership * If You Want Success, Lead Like This* Author Glen Aubrey (Creative Team Publishing) https://creativeteampublishing.com

*See You at the Top* by Author Zig Ziglar (Pelican Publishing) http://www.pelicanpublishing.com

# About the Author

Mark Chrysler was born in San Diego, California in 1960. His was a Navy family. At a young age, Mark and the family departed San Diego and moved to the Philippines. They lived in Navy housing in Subic Bay.

Later the family relocated back to the United States. After his mother divorced and eventually remarried a wonderful man, Mark's family bought a home in a small rural town called Dorr, Michigan. Go Blue!

During the summer after his high school senior year, Mark made his move back to San Diego. After graduation, on a dare from a family friend, he worked for a time in Bakersfield, California at a carrot packaging plant.

Mark soon learned one of his first valuable life lessons. It was that people have more to offer than the work they perform. He learned how important it is to look past just the job description.

In the fall of 1979, Mark began his college experience. In the spring of 1980, Mark and his best friend struck out to make their first million, starting a courier/office supply business in Denver, Colorado. Why not? The prospects of being a business owner were way more exciting than being a college student.

His second life lesson soon was revealed. It was this: there is no free lunch in life, and many of the people you meet do not subscribe to the philosophy of "my word is my bond." After working odd jobs, Mark was offered what became his career steppingstone. He became an apprentice electrician for his girlfriend's dad's electrical contracting company. Mark and his girlfriend became engaged and married on March 30, 1985. In 1988, their son was born; in 1990, their daughter was born.

Mark and his wife have been married over 37 years. Mark retired as a Senior Electrical Inspector for the City of San Diego.

*****

**Note**: The following is the meaning of the <u>acrostic graphic</u> on the back cover. **A**: Authentic; **H**: Hope; **C**: Commands; **S**: Surrender. Interestingly, as one embraces a life receptive to the message of *Authentic Hope*, submission to God's commands is more like accepting a warm and loving invitation to a relationship where all other relationships pale in comparison.

*****

# The Publisher and Printer

o   **Creative Team Publishing**
    (CTP www.creativeteampublishing.com) was
    formed in 2007.
o   **Creative Team Resources Group**
    (CTRG www.ctrg.com) began in the early 1980s
    and is the parent company, and the exclusive
    owner of CTP.

Publishing printed books, paperback, and hardback, is at
the heart of the business and ministry entities. Our printer is
Lightning Source/Ingram with locations in the United States
and other international locations as well.

It has been an honor to do business with them since 2014.
Contact information:

Lightning Source Inc. (US)
1246 Heil Quaker Blvd.
La Vergne, TN USA 37086
Email: inquiry@lightningsource.com
Voice: 1-800-509-4156

*****

CPSIA information can be obtained
at www.ICGtesting.com
Printed in the USA
BVHW041205160423
662436BV00004B/143

9 780985 597948